The of Bracken Cave

by Christine Griffith

PEARSON

Glenview, Illinois • Boston, Massachusetts
Chandler, Arizona • Upper Saddle River, New Jersey

An Amazing Sight

Just outside of San Antonio, Texas, something amazing happens each summer night. Dark shapes fly from a cave. At first, there are just a few. Soon there are many shapes leaving the cave. The shapes begin to spin up into the air like a tornado. Soon the evening sky becomes a dark cloud of flapping wings. For the next several hours, the shapes fly from the cave. They move out across the Texas sky. These are the bats of Bracken Cave.

This might sound scary. However, these bats have an important role in the Texas ecosystem. Each night, the bats leave their cave in search of insects. They eat thousands of pounds of harmful insects every night. They help farmers by controlling pests that harm crops.

---

ecosystem: a group of living things that work together

Bats leave Bracken Cave at night.

▲ Bracken Cave is near San Antonio, a large city in Texas.

◀ From spring until fall, bats leave the cave each night to hunt for insects.

How Bats Get to Bracken Cave

Bracken Cave is in central Texas, just 20 miles from San Antonio. Every year, millions of Mexican free-tailed bats migrate. They go from Mexico to the southern and western areas of the United States. Each spring, the bats fly north to Texas. Each fall, they return to Mexico. Some bats fly over 1,000 miles during their migration.

---

migrate: to move from one place to another

▲ Mexican free-tailed bat

▶ Mexican free-tailed bats are furry.

Why Bats Live in Bracken Cave

Many of the bats that migrate live in groups called *colonies.* More than 20 million Mexican free-tailed bats live in the colony in Bracken Cave. Most of the Mexican free-tailed bats that migrate to Bracken Cave are female. These bats migrate to Texas to have their babies. The bats need warm caves. They also need a safe place to sleep during the day. Most of all, the bats need a large supply of food.

The area around Bracken Cave provides plenty of food. When the bats leave the cave, they rise up into the air. Sometimes they reach a height of 10,000 feet. High in the air, they find migrating insects. Insects provide the bats with food.

What Bats Are Like

Bats fly like birds, but they are not birds. Instead, they are part of a group of animals called *mammals*. People, dogs, and horses are other examples of mammals. All mammals have hair and warm blood.

Most mammal babies grow inside their mothers and are born alive. They do not grow inside eggs the way that birds, fish, or snakes do. All mammals also nurse their young. After the babies are born, the bat mothers feed milk to their babies. The babies are called pups.

MAMMALS	BIRDS	REPTILES
• Have hair or fur	• Have feathers	• Have scales
• Give birth to live young • Nurse their young	• Lay eggs	• Lay eggs
• Warm-blooded	• Warm-blooded	• Cold-blooded

nurse: to care for and feed with milk

Bats hang upside down from the walls of caves.

Bats are *nocturnal*. This means that they sleep during the day and become active at night. During the day, the bats of Bracken Cave sleep by hanging from the walls of the cave. The bats hang upside down.

Bats have a special way of finding their food at night. A bat makes a special sound that is so high, it can't be heard by humans. These sounds travel in ==waves== through the air. When the waves hit an object, they bounce back to the bat. This helps the bat "see" where things are. The bats can avoid hitting things. They can also find and grab the flying insects they eat.

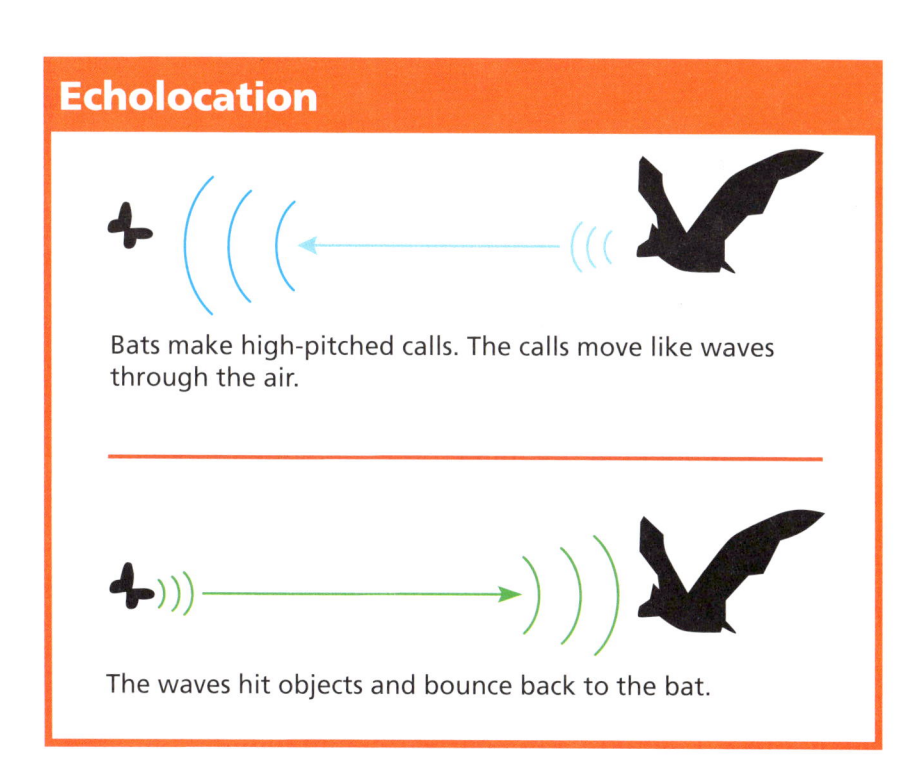

Echolocation

Bats make high-pitched calls. The calls move like waves through the air.

The waves hit objects and bounce back to the bat.

---

waves: movements through the air that carry sound from one place to another

Baby bats and a mother bat

How Bats Raise Their Young

Mexican free-tailed bats spend their winters in Mexico. The bats arrive at Bracken Cave in March or April. By late June, female bats give birth to single pups. After the birth of the babies, there are almost 40 million bats in the cave.

After a baby bat is born, its mother spends about an hour learning its smell and sounds. This helps the mother bat find her baby among millions of others in the cave. Mother bats nurse their babies twice a day. The mothers need to eat a lot of insects to be able to feed their babies.

Think about how much you weigh. Then imagine eating the same weight of food in just one day. Mother bats eat more than their own weight in insects in one day.

Up to 500 baby bats fit into a space that is 12 inches long and 12 inches wide.

The bat pups roost in a different part of the cave, away from their mothers. The tiny bats cling to the cave wall. As many as 500 bat pups can fit into just one square foot of space. That's about the same size as the cover of a large book. Staying close together helps keep the baby bats warm.

Bat pups learn to fly when they are four to five weeks old. They practice by dropping off the cave wall. The bats flip in the air and land back on the wall a few seconds later. But they must be careful. If they fall, insects on the ground might eat them.

---

roost: live and sleep

How Bats Help People

When the bats come out of Bracken Cave at night, they fly many miles in search of food. The bats look for insects. Mexican free-tailed bats eat moths that destroy cotton, corn, and other farm crops. These pests cause a billion dollars of damage every year. The bats also eat biting insects like mosquitoes.

Moths like these can hurt crops.

Mosquitoes bite people and can spread sickness.

Twenty million bats or more can eat a lot of insects every night. Bracken Cave bats eat approximately 200 tons, or about 400,000 pounds, of insects each night. Without the help of bats, even more crops might be harmed. Farmers also need fewer chemicals to kill the insect pests.

Extend Language **Bat Facts**

- Bats are the only mammals that can fly.
- The bat colony at Bracken Cave is the largest community of mammals on Earth.
- Bats are not blind. They can see well.

▲ San Antonio is one of the largest cities in the United States.

▶ Bat Conservation International bought the land around Bracken Cave to protect it.

Why Bracken Cave Needs Protection

More than one million people live in the city of San Antonio. It is the seventh-largest city in the United States. With so many people, much of the land around the city has been developed. New houses, offices, and shopping malls have been built all around the city.

To protect Bracken Cave, an organization called Bat Conservation International has bought 700 acres of land surrounding the cave. The group wants to keep the land safe. They do not want to disturb the bats. The group is trying to restore the land to the way it was hundreds of years ago. They also plan to build a visitor center. People who are curious about Bracken Cave bats can go to the center to learn more about them.

---

restore: make something the way it was in the past